Parenting for Academic Success
A Curriculum for Families Learning English

Unit 11:
Reading Aloud to Your Child
PARENT WORKBOOK

Lesson 1: Reading Aloud

Lesson 2: Selecting Children's Books

National Center for Family Literacy

Copyright © 2005 by the National Center for Family Literacy

All rights reserved. No part of this publication may be reproduced or transmitted in any form or by any means, electronic or mechanical, including photocopying, recording, or any information storage and retrieval system, without permission in writing from the publisher.

Requests for permission to make copies of any part of the work should be sent to:

DELTA PUBLISHING COMPANY
A Divison of DELTA PUBLISHING GROUP
1400 Miller Parkway
McHenry, IL 60050 USA
(800) 323-8270 or (815) 363-3582
www.delta-systems.com

Printed in the United States of America

Parent Workbook 11   ISBN-10: 1-932748-39-3
                     ISBN-13: 978-1-932748-39-0

Acknowledgments

Parenting for Academic Success: A Curriculum for Families Learning English was developed by the National Center for Family Literacy (NCFL) in collaboration with the Center for Applied Linguistics (CAL) and K. Lynn Savage, English as a Second Language (ESL) Teacher and Training Consultant.

Principle Curriculum Authors: Janet M. Fulton (NCFL), Laura Golden (CAL), Dr. Betty Ansin Smallwood (CAL), and K. Lynn Savage, Educational Consultant.

Special thanks to the Toyota Family Literacy Program, which piloted these materials in Washington, DC; New York, NY; Providence, RI; Chicago, IL; and Los Angeles, CA.

The Verizon Foundation provided original funding for the development of this curriculum and supports the National Center for Family Literacy in its development of resources for English language learners. Verizon's support of the literacy cause includes Thinkfinity.org, a free digital learning platform that advances learning in traditional settings and beyond the classroom. Visit the Thinkfinity Literacy Network managed by the National Center for Family Literacy and ProLiteracy Worldwide on Thinkfinity.org for free online courses and resources that support literacy across the life span.

Special thanks to Jennifer McMaster (NCFL) for her editing expertise.

A Message for Parents

This program is designed for parents who want to build their English language skills. The program also will help you learn ways to help your child improve his or her skills to succeed in school.

You will do activities to learn and practice reading, writing, speaking and listening in English. These activities also share information about how children learn to speak and read English. Each lesson has an activity you can do with your child at home.

When you support your child's learning at home, your child learns how language works.

Doing family learning activities together:

- Helps you be your child's first teacher.
- Helps you learn how your child learns.
- Makes learning fun.
- Supports your child's learning outside the classroom.

You can help your child learn every day. This program will help you help your child to learn.

Un Mensaje para Padres

Este programa está creado para padres que quieren mejorar sus destrezas en inglés. A la misma vez el programa les va a ayudar apoyar el aprendizaje de sus niños y a prepararlos para tener éxito escolar cuando entran a las escuelas.

Dentro encontrarán actividades para que mejoren sus destrezas de lectura, escritura, y conversación en inglés. Las actividades van a compartir información acerca de cómo aprenden los niños a hablar y leer en inglés. Cada lección tiene actividades para hacer en casa con sus niños.

Cuando usted apoya el aprendizaje de su niño en casa, él o ella aprende como se usa el lenguaje.

Cuando hacen actividades escolares juntos:

- Le ayuda ser el primer maestro de su niño.
- Le ayuda aprender como aprende su niño.
- Aprendiendo conceptos es más divertido.
- Apoya el aprendizaje de su niño fuera del salón de clase.

Le puede ayudar a su niño diariamente. Este programa le ayuda apoyar el aprendizaje de su niño.

LESSON 1

 **Lesson 1: Reading Aloud**

Lesson Goal
Learn how to read aloud with your child at home to support his or her language and literacy development.

Lesson Objectives
Today we will:

▸ Listen to and enjoy storybooks and reading aloud.

▸ Share experiences about reading aloud.

▸ Learn and practice reading aloud stages.

▸ Prepare to read aloud with your child at home.

Lesson Warm–up

1. Circle *yes* or *no* or make a check (✔) in the box to answer the questions.

▸ Did anyone read to you as a child?   Yes   No

▸ Who read to you?

My _____ read to me.

☐ mother	☐ sister or brother	☐ priest, minister, rabbi
☐ father	☐ teacher (can you remember a name?)	or other religious leader
☐ grandparent		

▸ How often did someone read to you?

Someone read to me _____.

| ☐ every day | ☐ once a week | ☐ once a year |
| ☐ every two or three days | ☐ once a month | |

▸ What did he or she read?

He or she read _____ to me.

| ☐ picture books | ☐ newspapers | ☐ advertisements |
| ☐ storybooks | ☐ magazines | ☐ other things |

LESSON 1

▶ What do you remember about the experience?

   I remember _____ .

   ☐ a special book   ☐ a special place
   ☐ a special person   ☐ a special time

2. Read these questions. What do you think? Share your ideas.

   ▶ Why should you read to your child?
   _____

   ▶ How often should you read to your child?
   _____

   ▶ What should you read?
   _____

   ▶ What can you do to make reading a good learning experience?
   _____

Points to Remember

Use reading strategies before, during and after you read aloud to your child. It will help you and your child:

- ▶ Develop vocabulary skills.
- ▶ Strengthen language and communication skills.
- ▶ Develop listening skills.
- ▶ Share feelings of trust, security and pleasure.

Can you add some more important points to this list?

_____
_____
_____
_____

LESSON 1

 ACTIVITY 1: Key Vocabulary

Words in this lesson are listed below. Use the Key Vocabulary pages to build your vocabulary.

1. Review the words. Which ones do you know?

Word Part	Word	Example	Translation
noun	author		
noun	illustrator		
noun	title		
verb	choose		
verb	picture read		
verb	preview		
verb	review		
verb	select		
preposition	after		
preposition	before		
preposition	during		

UNIT 11: Reading Aloud to Your Child

LESSON 1

2. Practice Key Vocabulary words. Write the Tic–Tac–Toe vocabulary words below.

Word: Sentence:	Word: Sentence:	Word: Sentence:
Word: Sentence:	Word: Sentence:	Word: Sentence:
Word: Sentence:	Word: Sentence:	Word: Sentence:

3. Practice Key Vocabulary words. Write three sentences with three Key Vocabulary words.

   Example: *I like to read before I go to bed.*

   _____

   _____.

   _____

   _____.

   _____

   _____.

LESSON 1

ACTIVITY 2: Before Reading Aloud

1. Listen while your teacher demonstrates "*before* reading aloud" strategies.

2. Answer these preview questions. Look at the book cover.

    ▸ What is the title? The title is _____.

    ▸ Who is the author? The author is _____.

    ▸ Who is the illustrator? The illustrator is _____.

3. Answer these prediction questions. Read the book title.

    ▸ What is the story is about?

    The story is about _____.

    ▸ What clues (words or pictures) give you those ideas?

    _____
    _____.

4. Answer these "picture read" questions. Follow these steps.
    ▸ Look at the pictures and illustrations inside the book.
    ▸ Look at words printed in dark or bold type inside the book.
    ▸ Define or translate any new words and add them to your Key Vocabulary.
    ▸ Make more predictions.

    What helped you make predictions?

    _____

    Did your predictions change after the picture read?

    _____

5. Practice "*before* reading aloud" strategies with a partner.
    ▸ Preview the book cover.
    ▸ Make predictions from the book cover and book title.
    ▸ "Picture read" and talk about words in the book.

UNIT 11: Reading Aloud to Your Child

LESSON 1

Activity 3: During Reading Aloud

1. Listen while your teacher demonstrates reading with expression. Then, answer these questions.

    ▸ How did your teacher use his or her voice, face and body?

    _____

    _____

    ▸ How did this help express meaning?

    _____

    _____

2. Read these tips for reading aloud with expression.
    ▸ Read slowly.
    ▸ Read some parts loudly and some parts softly.
    ▸ Act out different parts.

3. Read a book with expression. First, practice by yourself. Then, practice with a partner. Follow these steps.
    ▸ Read aloud with expression.
    ▸ Talk about the pictures.
    ▸ Stop and ask a question about what happened.
    ▸ Ask what might happen next.

LESSON 1

ACTIVITY 4: After Reading Aloud

1. Listen while your teacher demonstrates "*after* reading" strategies. List the strategies.
    ▶ Write three "*after* reading" strategies.

    _____

    _____

    _____

2. Review these "*after* reading" strategies. Which ones do you use? Circle them.

    Reflect.
    Ask yourself these questions:

    ▶ What do you think of the book? How did it make you feel?

    ▶ Did you like it? Why? Why not?

    ▶ What parts did you like? What was your favorite part? Why?

    Check Your Understanding.
    Follow these steps. Ask yourself these questions:

    ▶ Check your predictions. Did your predictions match the story?

    ▶ What happened in the story? Check for understanding (comprehension).

    ▶ What was the main idea?

    ▶ What are some ideas in the book? Do you agree with them?

    ▶ How does this book remind you of other books, family stories, traditions or your own experience?

    Extend Your Learning.
    Do these activities after you read the story:

    ▶ Draw your favorite part of the story. Write some words or a sentence about your picture.

    ▶ Write new words or ideas learned from the story.

    ▶ Write a journal reflection about the story. (Teachers sometimes call these "literature logs.")

    ▶ Retell or reread the story. (Children often ask for their favorite story to be reread many times!)

    ▶ Change the story. For example, make up a different ending.

    ▶ Plan an activity from an idea in the story.

3. Practice "*after* reading" strategies with a partner. Take turns practicing these strategies.
    ▶ Reflect.
    ▶ Check your understanding.
    ▶ Extend your learning.

LESSON 1

ACTIVITY 5: Think About Today's Lesson

1. Reflect on what you learned. Finish the sentences.

    Today I learned _____

    _____

    _____

    _____.

    I plan to _____

    _____

    _____

    _____.

    A question I still have is _____

    _____

    _____

    _____.

2. Reflect on some important ideas and vocabulary words you heard in this lesson.
    ▸ Read the words below.
    ▸ With the class, talk about these words.
    ▸ Add any new words you want to remember below.

    - preview
    - picture read
    - predict
    - reflect
    - extend
    -
    -
    -

LESSON 1

3. Review the ideas in the lesson.

   Lesson 1: Reading Aloud

   ▸ Name three reading aloud strategies.

   1. _____.
   2. _____.
   3. _____.

   ▸ Identify things you can do *before* reading aloud.

   1. _____.
   2. _____.
   3. _____.

   ▸ Identify things you can do *during* reading aloud.

   1. _____.
   2. _____.
   3. _____.

   ▸ Identify things you can do *after* reading aloud.

   1. _____.
   2. _____.
   3. _____.

**Why Reading Aloud to Children Is Important
Ten Reasons**

Reading aloud to your child:
1. Gives time to be close and cuddle with your child.
2. Helps children read books in your home language and English.
3. Develops language and listening skills.
4. Increases vocabulary and builds knowledge.
5. Takes less than 15 minutes per day.
6. Provides time to share family stories and ideas about books.
7. Is free.
8. Lets children experience different kinds of books.
9. Provides experience in previewing, predicting and reflecting.
10. Helps children become better readers and writers.

LESSON 1

4. Do you have any other important ideas you learned from this lesson?
    - List them below.
    - Share your ideas with the class.

    _____

    _____

    _____

    _____

LESSON 1

 Take–Home Activity

LESSON 1: Reading Aloud

Goal
Read with your child using read aloud strategies practiced in class.

Objectives

- Select a book with your child to read aloud.
- Preview, predict, "picture read" and talk about words before you read.
- Read slowly and with expression.
- Check for understanding (comprehension).
- Extend your child's learning after you read together.

Directions

1. Prepare. Review the reading aloud strategies you practiced in class. Then, plan ahead.

    - Choose a book to read in either English or your home language.
    - Preview it before you read it with your child.
    - Find a quiet place to read.
    - Plan 15 minutes when you can read with your child without interruptions.

2. Try this at home.

    - Read aloud with your child.
        - Sit close or let your child sit in your lap.
        - Cuddle! Giggle! Learn together!
        - Get your child excited about the book. Ask questions.
        - Let your child turn the pages and tell a story about the pictures as you read.
        - Enjoy your special time together!

LESSON 1

3. Review.
   - ▶ Think about the things you did with your child.
   - ▶ Write answers or make some notes.

   What is the title of one book you read aloud to your child?
   _____

   What did you do *before* reading aloud?
   _____.

   What did you do *during* reading aloud?
   _____.

   What did you do *after* reading aloud?
   _____.

4. Reflect.
   - ▶ What did you and your child have fun doing?

     We had fun _____
     _____.

   - ▶ What do you think your child learned?

     My child learned _____
     _____.

   - ▶ What went well?
     _____
     _____ went well.

   - ▶ What could go better next time?
     _____
     _____ could go better next time.

Parenting for Academic Success

LESSON 1

 Actividad para realizar en el hogar

Lección 1: Cómo leer en voz alta

Meta
Leer con los niños utilizando las estrategias de leer en voz alta que practicó en clase.

Objetivos

- Seleccionar un libro con su niño que puedan leer en voz alta.
- Repasar, predecir, leer las ilustraciones y conversar sobre las palabras antes de leer.
- Leer lentamente y con expresión.
- Confirmar que su niño entienda (comprenda).
- Ampliar el aprendizaje del niño después de la lectura.

Instrucciones

1. Prepárese. Repasa las estrategias de leer en voz alta que practicaron en clase y luego haga un plan.

    - Seleccione un libro que pueda leer en inglés o en su lengua materna.
    - Revíselo y mírelo con anticipación.
    - Escoja un lugar tranquilo para leer.
    - Planifique 15 minutos durante los cuales pueda leer sin interrupciones con su niño.

2. Para hacer en casa.

    - Lean en voz alta usted y su niño.
        - Siéntese cerca del niño o déjelo que se siente en su regazo.
        - ¡Acurrúquense! ¡Ríanse! ¡Aprendan juntos!
        - Anime al niño con el libro. Hágale preguntas.
        - Deje que él o ella dé vuelta a las páginas y cuente una historia sobre las ilustraciones a medida va leyendo.
        - ¡Disfruten estos momentos tan especiales juntos!

UNIT 11: Reading Aloud to Your Child

LESSON 1

3. Repase.
    ▶ Piense en lo que hizo con su niño.
    ▶ Escriba las respuestas o tome apuntes.

    ¿Cuál es el título de uno de los libros que le leo a su niño en voz alta?
    _____

    ¿Qué hizo *antes* de leerle en voz alta?
    _____.

    ¿Qué hizo *mientras* le leía en voz alta?
    _____.

    ¿Qué hizo *después* de leerle?
    _____.

4. Reflexione.
    ▶ ¿Con qué actividad se divirtieron más usted y su niño?
    Nos divertimos _____
    _____.

    ▶ ¿Qué cree que aprendió su niño?
    Mi niño aprendió _____
    _____.

    ▶ ¿Qué cosas resultaron bien?
    _____
    _____ resultaron bien.

    ▶ ¿Qué podría resultar mejor la próxima vez?
    _____
    _____ podría resultar mejor la próxima vez.

LESSON 2

 **Lesson 2: Selecting Children's Books**

Lesson Goal
Learn to identify and help your child select different types of children's books.

Lesson Objectives
Today we will:

- Identify different types of children's books.
- Practice how to choose books for your child.
- Prepare to select and read books aloud with your child.

Lesson Warm–Up

1. Circle your answers to these questions or statements.

    - Do you find reading easy or difficult?

        Easy   In between   Difficult

    - What language do you prefer to read in?

        English   My home language

    - I enjoy reading…

        A lot   Some   Not much

LESSON 2

2. Put a check (✔) in the right box. What kinds of things do you read?

I read	A lot	Some	Not much
magazines (which ones?)			
newspapers			
advertisements (what kind?)			
menus			
forms (for what?)			
bills			
letters			
e–mails			
the Bible or Koran (or other religious books)			
books (which ones?)			
other things?			

3. What is something interesting you read recently?

   I read _____

   _____

   _____.

4. Think, Pair, Share.
   ▶ Think about the questions. (*Think*)
   ▶ Discuss your answers with a partner. (*Pair*)
   ▶ Share your ideas with the class or in a small group. (*Share*)

   What do you know about your child's reading?

   a) Is reading easy or difficult for your child?

   _____
   _____
   _____

   b) What language does your child prefer to read in?

   _____
   _____
   _____

   c) Does your child enjoy reading?

   _____
   _____
   _____

   d) What things does your child like to read?

   _____
   _____
   _____

LESSON 2

 Points to Remember

Know and read different kinds—genres—of children's books. It will help you and your child:

- Learn how writing is used in different ways for different purposes.
- Learn language patterns important to reading development.
- Develop comprehension skills.

Can you add some more important points to this list?

_____

_____

_____

_____

LESSON 2

 ACTIVITY 1: Key Vocabulary

Words in this lesson are listed below. Use the Key Vocabulary pages to build your vocabulary.

1. Review the words. Which ones do you know?

Word Part	Word	Example	Translation
noun	chapter book		
noun	fiction		
noun	nonfiction		
noun	picture book		
noun	poetry		
noun	storybook		

2. Practice using Key Vocabulary words. Write four sentences with four Key Vocabulary words.

Example: *My son and I read from his favorite storybook at bedtime.*

_____
_____.
_____
_____.
_____
_____.
_____
_____.

UNIT 11: Reading Aloud to Your Child   19

LESSON 2

ACTIVITY 2: Identifying Children's Literature

1. Listen as your teacher talks about these types of children's books.

Types of children's books	Definitions	Examples
picture books		
wordless books		
alphabet and counting books		
singable books		
nursery rhymes		
fairy tales		
folk tales and legends		
beginning readers		
easy–to–read books		
beginning chapter books		
poetry and rhyme		
non–fiction and information books		
biographies		
autobiographies		

LESSON 2

2. Answer these questions.

    ▸ Which types of books do I like? Why?

    I like _____ because _____

    _____.

    ▸ Which types of books do I think my child will like? Why?

    My child will like _____ because _____

    _____.

3. Play a Mix and Match game. Follow your teacher's directions.

4. Take the cards home to play this game with your child.

LESSON 2

ACTIVITY 3: Types of Books

1. Draw a line between the *definitions* and the book *genres* that match. The first one is done as an example. (Hint: There is one correct match for each definition.)

   Definitions

   1. Books with pictures only

   2. True stories

   3. Books with letters or numbers

   4. First books children read on their own

   5. Books with music and repeated patterns

   6. Stories passed down orally

   7. Text with rhythm and rhyme

   8. True stories about people written by others

   9. Books that combine text and pictures

   10. Books that feature imaginary beings with magical powers

   Genre

   a. poetry and rhyme

   b. beginning readers

   c. wordless books

   d. singable books

   e. biographies

   f. folk tales

   g. non-fiction

   h. alphabet or counting books

   i. picture books

   j. fairy tales

2. Choose a genre and a book you like. Read it aloud with a partner.
   ▶ Look through books from different genres.
   ▶ Choose a book you like and you think your child will like.
   ▶ Find a partner with a book from the same genre.
   ▶ Take turns practicing the reading aloud strategies.
   ▶ Write a book title and genre you like.

   Title: _____

   Genre: _____

LESSON 2

ACTIVITY 4: Selecting Books for Reading Aloud

1. Read these guidelines for selecting books to read aloud. Ask and answer these questions when you choose books for your child.

    a) Do you like the book? Does it interest you?
    - If you like it, you can probably get your child excited about it.

    b) Do you think your child will like it?
    - If it matches your child's interests, your child will probably like it.

    c) Is the book visually attractive and appealing?
    - Look at the illustrations. Do the illustrations help explain the words and the story (this is important for English language learners)?
    - Look at the overall presentation. What is the size of print? How much information is on a page?

    d) Is the book at (or slightly above) your child's language level?
    - There is no right answer, only a right match.
    - Look at the number of words and amount of information on each page.
    - Look at the level of difficulty.
    - For beginning English language learners, select books with few words on a page and illustrations that help tell the story.

    e) Does the book "teach" your child about something new or important?
    - Look for books about your culture or other cultures.
    - Look for books with morals or values you believe in.

    f) Is it a hard or easy book for your child?
    - Hard books—ones that a parent or an older brother or sister reads to a child (picture books).
    - Easy books—one that your child can read on his or her own (beginning readers).
    - Select a balance between "easy" and "hard" books.

LESSON 2

2. Use the guidelines to help you select 2 or 3 books for your child. Write down the title and author of the books you think are a good match for your child.

Title: _____

Author: _____

Title: _____

Author: _____

Title: _____

Author: _____

3. Share your selections with a small group. Tell why you chose the books you did. Listen and learn from other parents' choices.

4. What's important when you choose books?
   Identify three guidelines for choosing books for your child that are important to you.

   ▶ _____
   _____
   _____

   ▶ _____
   _____
   _____

   ▶ _____
   _____
   _____

Activity 5: Think About Today's Lesson

1. Reflect on what you learned. Finish the sentences.

   Today I learned _____
   _____
   _____
   _____
   _____.

   I plan to _____
   _____
   _____
   _____
   _____.

   A question I still have is _____
   _____
   _____
   _____
   _____.

2. Reflect on some important ideas and vocabulary words you heard in this lesson.
   ▸ Read the word below.
   ▸ Add any new words you want to remember below.

   - genre
   -
   -
   -

LESSON 2

3. Review the ideas in the lesson.

   Lesson 2: Selecting Children's Books
   Sharing different types or genres of books with your child is important. By looking at and reading different kinds of print, your child learns that print has different purposes. Help your child select books that he or she will learn from and enjoy.

4. Do you have any other important ideas you learned from this lesson?
   - List them below.
   - Share your ideas with the class.

   _____

   _____

   _____

   _____

Take–Home Activity

Lesson 2: Selecting Children's Books

Goal
Learn about different book genres and help your child select books.

Objectives
▶ Choose books for your child using the selection criteria.

▶ Read aloud with your child.

Directions
1. Prepare. Think about what you learned.

   ▶ Review the different types of books (genres).
   - picture books (fiction)
   - picture books (non–fiction)
   - beginning readers
   - poetry

   ▶ Review the book selection questions.
   - Do you like the book? Does it interest you?
   - Do you think your child will like it?
   - Is the book visually attractive and appealing?
   - Is the book at (or slightly above) your child's language level?
   - Does the book "teach" your child about something new or important?
   - Is it a hard or easy book?

2. Try this at home.

   ▶ Plan a trip to a school library or public library with your child.
   - Find out the hours the library is open.
   - Look for a library that is close to you and that matches your schedule.
   - Decide how you will get there (by bus, by car, on foot).

   ▶ At the library, use the guidelines to select books with your child.
   - Select at least two "hard" books (for you to read to your child).
   - Select at least two "easy" books (for your child to read on his or her own).
   - Make sure you bring or get a library card, so you can check out (take home) the books.

LESSON 2

▶ Select some books to read aloud with your child and read them together.
- Review the stages and strategies of reading aloud in Lesson 1.
- Sit close to or let your child sit in your lap.
- Cuddle! Giggle! Learn together!
- Let your child turn the pages and tell stories about the book.
- Enjoy the book and your special time together!
- Talk about the "easy" book or books your child reads on his or her own. Why did your child choose the book? What did your child like about the book? What did he or she learn from the book?

3. Review.
After you spend time with your child, think about the following points. Review the information, write your answers and bring the following information to share with your classmates.

▶ What are the titles of two books you selected?

Easy book (your child can read on his or her own):

_____

Hard book (a book you read aloud with your child):

_____

▶ Name two types of books that your child enjoys.

_____

_____

▶ Name two selection criteria you found helpful.

_____

_____

▶ Write a sentence about identifying and selecting books with your child.

_____

_____.

▶ What would you do differently next time?

_____

_____

_____.

4. Reflect.

▸ What did you and your child have fun doing?

We had fun _____

_____.

▸ What do you think your child learned?

My child learned _____

_____.

▸ What went well?

_____

_____ went well.

LESSON 2

Actividad para realizar en el hogar

LECCIÓN 2: Cómo seleccionar libros infantiles

Meta
Aprender sobre los distintos géneros de libros y cómo ayudarle al niño a seleccionarlos.

Objetivos
▶ Escoja libros para su niño utilizando los criterios de selección.

▶ Leer en voz alta con su niño.

Instrucciones
1. Prepárese. Piense en lo que aprendio.

    ▶ Repase los distintos tipos de libros (géneros).
    - libros con ilustraciones (ficción)
    - libros no con ilustraciones que no son ficción
    - lectores principiantes
    - poesía

    ▶ Repase las preguntas sobre la selección de los libros.
    - ¿Le gusta el libro? ¿Le interesa?
    - ¿Cree que le va a gustar a su niño?
    - ¿Es atractivo el libro?
    - ¿Está el libro al nivel (o levemente sobre el nivel) de lenguaje de su niño?
    - ¿Le "enseña" algo nuevo o importante el libro?
    - ¿Es un libro fácil o difícil?

2. Para hacer en casa.

    ▶ Programe un viaje con su niño a la biblioteca de la escuela o a la biblioteca pública.
    - Averigüe cuáles son las horas de atención de la biblioteca.
    - Busque una biblioteca que este cerca y que tengan un horario que coincida con el suyo.
    - Decida cómo llegará allí (en autobús, en automóvil, a caminando).

    ▶ Cuando llegue a la biblioteca, utilice las siguientes direcciones para seleccionar los libros con su niño.
    - Escoja por lo menos dos libros "difíciles" (para que se los lea usted al niño).
    - Escoja por lo menos dos libros "fáciles" (que su niño pueda leer solo).
    - Asegúrese de llevar u obtener una tarjeta para la biblioteca, para que pueda sacar (llevar a casa) los libros.

▸ Lea con el niño los libros que ustedes dos seleccionaron.
- Repase las etapas y las estrategias de la lectura en voz alta que aparecen en la Lección 1.
- Siéntese cerca de su niño, o deje que el niño se siente en su regazo.
- ¡Acurrúquense! ¡Ríanse! ¡Aprendan juntos!
- Deje que el niño dé vuelta a las páginas y cuente las historias sobre el libro.
- ¡Disfruten el libro y el tiempo tan especial que han pasado juntos!
- Converse con su niño sobre el libro o los libros "fáciles" que leyeron sin ayuda. ¿Por qué escogió el niño ese libro? ¿Qué es lo que más le gustó al niño sobre el libro? ¿Qué cosas aprendió el niño de éste?

3. Repase.
Después que haya pasado tiempo con su niño, piense en los puntos que siguen. Repase la información, escriba sus respuestas y traiga la información para que la comparta con sus compañeros.

▸ ¿Cuáles son los títulos de los dos libros que seleccionaron?

Libro fácil (que su niño puede leer sin ayuda):
_____

Libro difícil (que usted lee en voz alta a su niño):
_____

▸ Nombre dos tipos de libros que disfruta su niño.
_____
_____

▸ Nombre dos criterios de selección que usted consideró fueron más útiles.
_____
_____

▸ Escriba una oración que explique cómo identificar y seleccionar libros con su niño.
_____
_____.

▸ ¿Qué haría de otra forma la próxima vez?
_____
_____.

LESSON 2

4. Reflexione.

   ▶ ¿Con qué actividad se divirtieron más usted y su niño?

   Nos divertimos _____

   _____.

   ▶ ¿Qué cree que aprendió su niño?

   Mi niño aprendió _____

   _____.

   ▶ ¿Qué cosas resultaron bien?

   _____

   _____ resultaron bien.

Parent Survey

This survey is to evaluate the unit on **Reading Aloud to Your Child**. There are no wrong answers and you will not be asked to talk about your answers.

1. What information did you learn from the Reading Aloud to Your Child unit?

   _____

   _____

   _____

2. What else would you like to know about the Reading Aloud to Your Child unit?

   _____

   _____

   _____

3. How will the information help you help your child?

   _____

   _____

   _____

4. Check (✔) one of the following statements about this unit.

   _____ I understood everything.

   _____ I understood most of it.

   _____ I understood some of it.

   _____ I understood a little of it.

   _____ I did not understand any of it.

   When you have finished this survey, please give it to your teacher.

UNIT 11: Reading Aloud to Your Child

Encuesta a los padres

Esta encuesta es para evaluar la unidad de **Leerle en voz alta al niño**. No existen respuestas incorrectas y no se le pedirá que comente lo que respondió.

1. ¿Qué cosas aprendió en la unidad de Leerle en voz alta al niño?

   _____
   _____
   _____

2. ¿Qué otras cosas le gustarían saber acerca de la unidad de Leerle en voz alta al niño?

   _____
   _____
   _____

3. ¿De qué manera le ayudará a usted esta información para poder ayudar a su niño?

   _____
   _____
   _____

4. Marque (✔) sólo una de las siguientes afirmaciones sobre esta unidad.

   _____ Entendí todo.

   _____ Entendí la mayoría de las cosas.

   _____ Entendí algunas cosas.

   _____ Entendí un poco.

   _____ No entendí en absoluto.

   Cuando haya finalizado esta encuesta, entréguesela a su maestro.